SONGS FOR TWO

T0081899

Disney Characters and Artwork
TM & © 2018 Disney

*TARZAN® Owned by Edgar Rice Burroughs, Inc.
And Used by Permission
© Burroughs/Disney

The following songs are the property of:

Bourne Co.
Music Publishers
5 West 37th Street
New York, NY 10018

HEIGH-HO
SOME DAY MY PRINCE WILL COME
WHEN YOU WISH UPON A STAR
WHISTLE WHILE YOU WORK
WHO'S AFRAID OF THE BIG BAD WOLF?

Arrangements by Mark Phillips

ISBN 978-1-5400-3711-4

Visit Hal Leonard Online at
www.halleonard.com

Contact Us:
Hal Leonard
7777 West Bluemound Road
Milwaukee, WI 53213
Email: info@halleonard.com

In Europe contact:
Hal Leonard Europe Limited
42 Wigmore Street
Marylebone, London, W1U 2RN
Email: info@halleonardeurope.com

In Australia contact:
Hal Leonard Australia Pty. Ltd.
4 Lentara Court
Cheltenham, Victoria, 3192 Australia
Email: info@halleonard.com.au

BEAUTY AND THE BEAST
from BEAUTY AND THE BEAST

TRUMPETS

Music by ALAN MENKEN
Lyrics by HOWARD ASHMAN

Moderately slow

BIBBIDI-BOBBIDI-BOO

(The Magic Song)

from CINDERELLA

TRUMPETS

Words by JERRY LIVINGSTON
Music by MACK DAVID
and AL HOFFMAN

CAN YOU FEEL THE LOVE TONIGHT

from THE LION KING

TRUMPETS

Music by ELTON JOHN
Lyrics by TIM RICE

Slowly, in 2

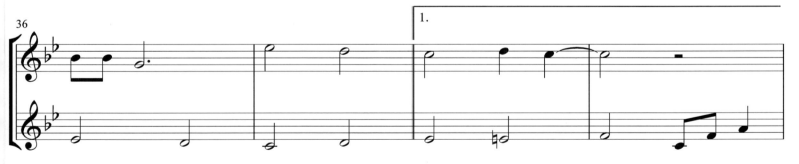

CHIM CHIM CHER-EE

from MARY POPPINS

TRUMPETS

Words and Music by RICHARD M. SHERMAN
and ROBERT B. SHERMAN

© 1964 Wonderland Music Company, Inc.
Copyright Renewed.
All Rights Reserved. Used by Permission.

CIRCLE OF LIFE

from THE LION KING

Music by ELTON JOHN
Lyrics by TIM RICE

TRUMPETS

Moderately slow

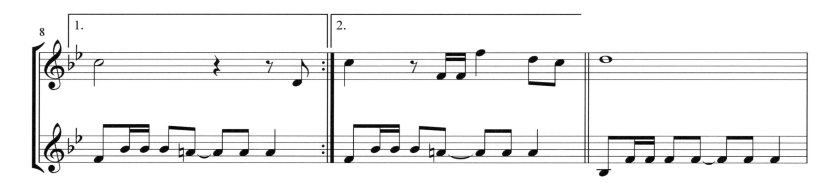

COLORS OF THE WIND

from POCAHONTAS

TRUMPETS

Music by ALAN MENKEN
Lyrics by STEPHEN SCHWARTZ

Moderately

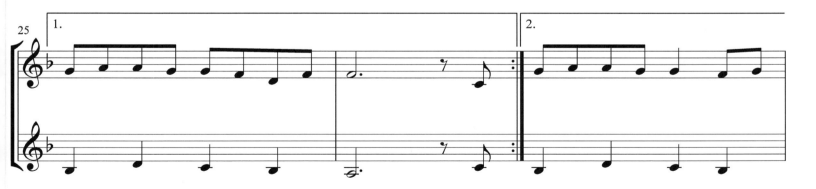

EVERMORE
from BEAUTY AND THE BEAST

TRUMPETS

Music by ALAN MENKEN
Lyrics by TIM RICE

Moderately

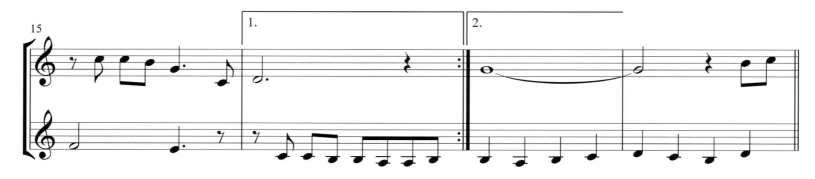

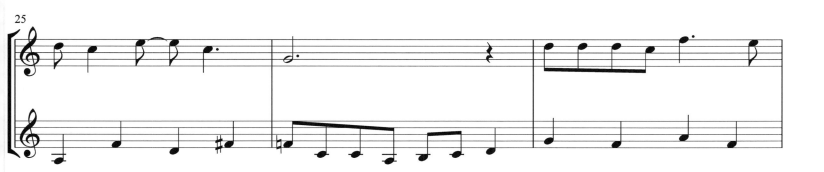

FRIEND LIKE ME

from ALADDIN

Music by ALAN MENKEN
Lyrics by HOWARD ASHMAN

TRUMPETS

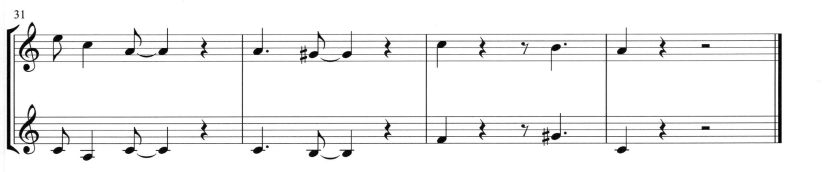

HEIGH-HO
The Dwarfs' Marching Song from SNOW WHITE AND THE SEVEN DWARFS

TRUMPETS

Words by LARRY MOREY
Music by FRANK CHURCHILL

Moderately, in 2

HOW FAR I'LL GO
from MOANA

TRUMPETS

Music and Lyrics by
LIN-MANUEL MIRANDA

Moderately, in 2

LET IT GO

from FROZEN

TRUMPETS

Music and Lyrics by KRISTEN ANDERSON-LOPEZ
and ROBERT LOPEZ

Slowly, in 2

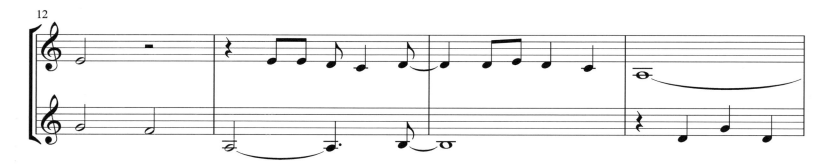

MICKEY MOUSE MARCH

from THE MICKEY MOUSE CLUB

TRUMPETS

Words and Music by
JIMMIE DODD

March tempo

SOME DAY MY PRINCE WILL COME

from SNOW WHITE AND THE SEVEN DWARFS

TRUMPETS

Words by LARRY MOREY
Music by FRANK CHURCHILL

Moderately

SOMETHING THERE

from BEAUTY AND THE BEAST

Music by ALAN MENKEN
Lyrics by HOWARD ASHMAN

TRUMPETS

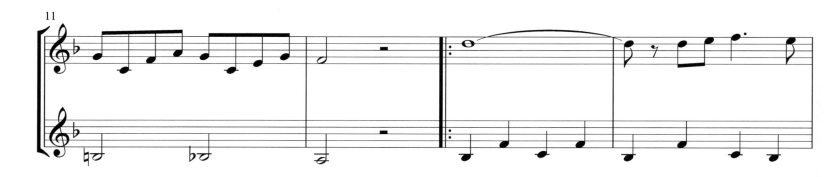

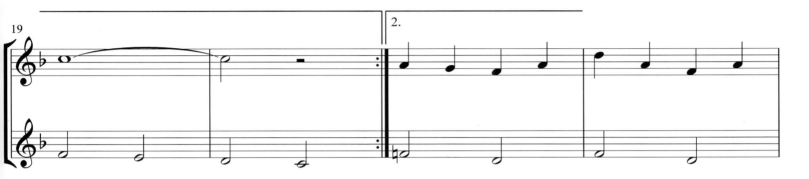

SUPERCALIFRAGILISTICEXPIALIDOCIOUS

from MARY POPPINS

TRUMPETS

Words and Music by RICHARD M. SHERMAN
and ROBERT B. SHERMAN

D.C. al Fine

WHEN SHE LOVED ME

from TOY STORY 2

TRUMPETS

Music and Lyrics by
RANDY NEWMAN

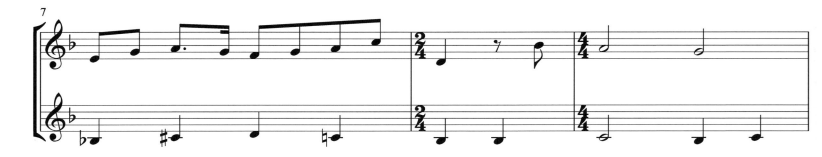

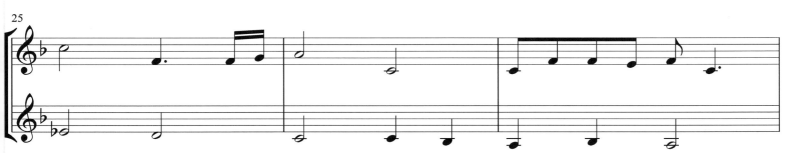

WHEN YOU WISH UPON A STAR

from PINOCCHIO

TRUMPETS

Words by NED WASHINGTON
Music by LEIGH HARLINE

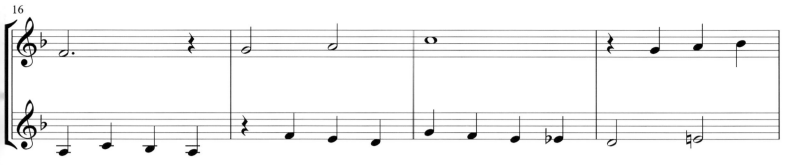

WHISTLE WHILE YOU WORK

from SNOW WHITE AND THE SEVEN DWARFS

Words by LARRY MOREY
Music by FRANK CHURCHILL

TRUMPETS

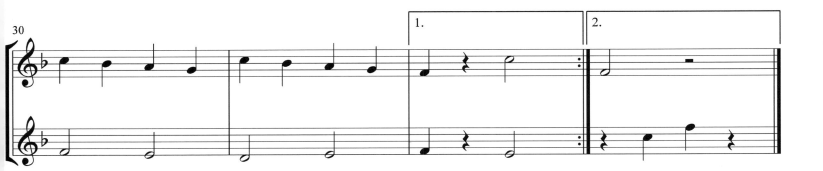

WHO'S AFRAID OF THE BIG BAD WOLF?

from THREE LITTLE PIGS

TRUMPETS

Words and Music by
FRANK CHURCHILL
Additional Lyric by ANN RONELL

Moderately, in 2

A WHOLE NEW WORLD

from ALADDIN

TRUMPETS

Music by ALAN MENKEN
Lyrics by TIM RICE

Moderately

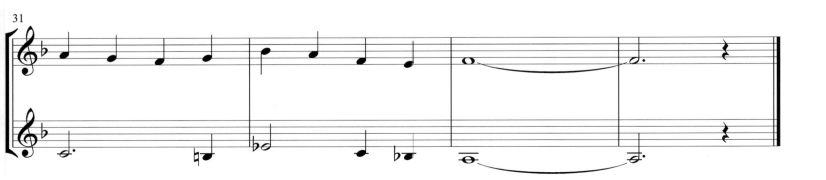

YOU'LL BE IN MY HEART

(Pop Version)

from TARZAN®

TRUMPETS

Words and Music by
PHIL COLLINS

Moderately

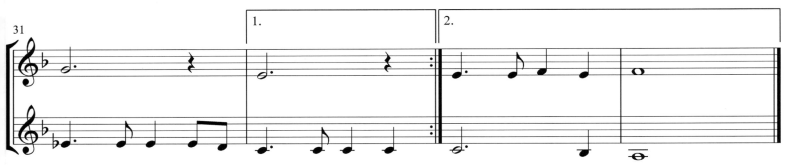

YOU'RE WELCOME

from MOANA

TRUMPETS

Music and Lyrics by
LIN-MANUEL MIRANDA

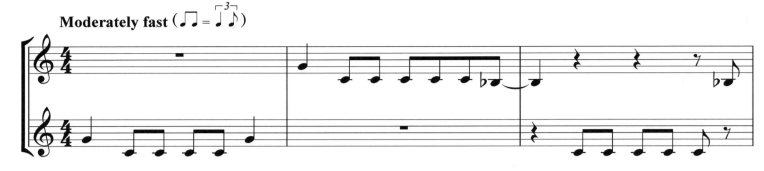

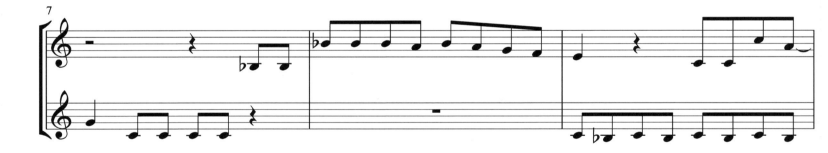

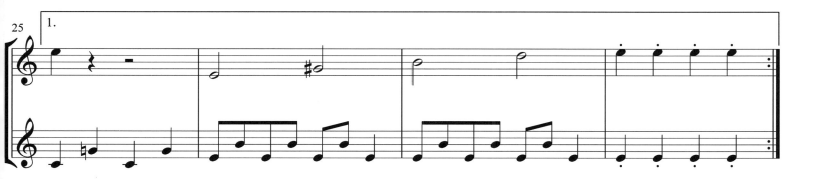

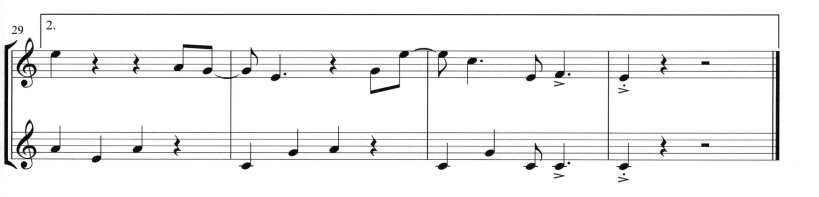

ZIP-A-DEE-DOO-DAH

from SONG OF THE SOUTH

TRUMPETS

Words by RAY GILBERT
Music by ALLIE WRUBEL